Secrets of the Desert

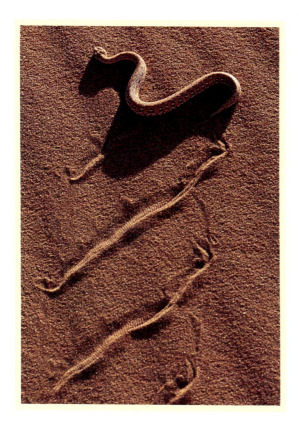

Kath Murdoch and Stephen Ray

You can find the definitions of **boldfaced** words used in this book on page 31.

Contents

WHAT ARE DESERTS? 4

LOTS OF LIFE 6

KEEPING COOL 10

SECRETS OF THE NIGHT 14

FINDING WATER 16

FINDING FOOD 18

SUDDEN HEAVY RAINS 20

DESERT POOLS 22

PEOPLE OF THE DESERT 24

DESERT DIGGINGS 26

WHERE ARE DESERTS? 28

WHO MADE THESE TRACKS? 30

GLOSSARY 31

INDEX 32

What are Deserts?

Deserts are places where water is **scarce**. They have very little rainfall, and most deserts are very hot during the day. In some deserts, the temperature of the ground can sometimes reach as high as 80°C. That's hot enough to burn you very badly. It's hard to imagine how any living thing could **survive** there.

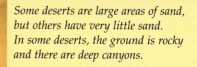

Some deserts are large areas of sand, but others have very little sand. In some deserts, the ground is rocky and there are deep canyons.

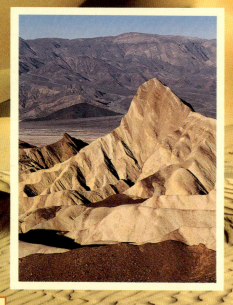

DESERT FACTS: COLD DESERTS?
Antarctica is an extremely cold place. But many scientists describe parts of it as desert because no rain has fallen there for hundreds of years.

Lots of Life

Animals and plants of the desert have little protection from the sun, and they must survive extreme temperatures and a lack of water. And yet there is an **enormous** variety of life that survives in these difficult conditions, from small bushes to huge **cacti**.

▲ *A sand lizard, Namib Desert, Africa*

▲ A colorful wildflower of the Great Victoria Desert, Australia

▲ A barrel **cactus**, Borrego Desert, North America

Can you guess whose tracks these are?

◀ A gemsbok, Namib Desert, Africa

Many desert **creatures** have relatives that live in places with very different conditions. For example, there are some kinds of foxes who live in the hot, dry **environment** of the desert, but there are other kinds that live in cool areas of Europe. Each **species** has special features which help it to survive in its **habitat**.

A desert coyote and a gray wolf are closely related, but their differences help them survive in very different environments.

Do you know whose tracks these are?

They look very similar, but a forest dragon and a western bearded dragon live in very different environments.

A green sea turtle and a desert tortoise

Keeping Cool

In the middle of the day, when the temperature is at its highest, there are not many signs of life in the desert. Most animals escape the burning rays of the sun by staying in small areas of shade. Some animals have developed unusual ways to keep cool.

Dingoes pant to keep cool. The rapid movement of air over the tongue helps to cool the animal's blood.

Chameleons, like many desert reptiles, often stand on only two legs. Then they have less contact with the hot ground.

DESERT FACTS: WHY ARE DAYS SO HOT?
There are not many clouds over deserts, and there is very little moisture in desert air. This means that the sun's rays beat straight down, making the ground and the surrounding air very hot.

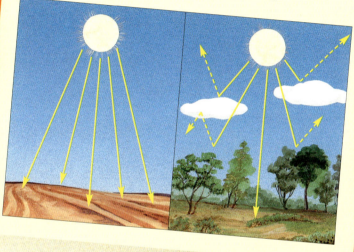

Can you guess what kind of creature left these tracks?

There is also life under the burning **surfaces** of many deserts. Some animals dig underground burrows. Burrows are protected from the direct rays of the sun, so they make cool homes.

The African golden mole is almost ▶ completely blind, and it uses its sense of touch to find its way in dark underground burrows.

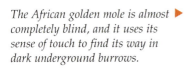

American spadefoot toads spend almost all of their lives under the ground. They come to the surface only after heavy rains.
▼

Termites

A termite mound

DESERT FACTS: LAYERS OF HEAT

The desert is hottest at the surface. Temperatures are lower above and below ground level.

- 300m 27°C
- 2m 43°C
- 1m 50°C
- Surface 75°C
- 1.5m 27°C

Some species of termites have a way of cooling their tall nest mounds. Below the mound, they build rows of thin walls which pull cooler underground air up into it.

13

Secrets of the Night

There are many changes in the desert at night. The desert becomes very cold because there are no clouds to hold in the day's heat. Many animals return to burrows, rocks, and bushes to stay warm and safe until morning, while **nocturnal animals** come out of their hiding places.

Elf owls are excellent nocturnal hunters.

▲ The thick coat of the fennec fox keeps it warm as it hunts in the cold night.

Gerbils come out of their burrows during the cool night.

▲ Evening primrose flowers would die if they opened in the daytime desert heat. In the cold night, the pale petals attract insects which help to **pollinate** the plant.

Finding Water

Like all living things, desert plants and animals must have water to survive. But water is usually very scarce in the desert – sometimes years pass without a drop of rain. Desert plants and animals have developed many ways to find and store the water they need to survive.

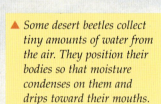

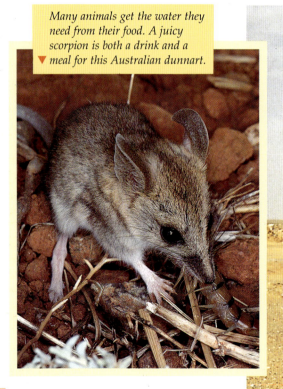

Many animals get the water they need from their food. A juicy scorpion is both a drink and a ▼ meal for this Australian dunnart.

▲ Some desert beetles collect tiny amounts of water from the air. They position their bodies so that moisture condenses on them and drips toward their mouths.

◀ The baobab tree stores water in its thick trunk.

Can you guess whose tracks these are?

Camels store fat in their humps. The fat is changed to liquid and energy as the camels need it.
▼

Finding Food

Desert creatures, like all animals, need to eat plants or other animals. But in the desert, plants and animals can be hard to find.

Desert animals can't afford to waste any food. Some animals eat not only the tasty leaves and fruit of plants but even the tough outer parts. Insects and other animals that live in and around desert plants become food for **predators**, too.

▲
Some desert animals eat only occasionally. If this sand snake eats the lizard, it will not need any more food for several days.

The saguaro cactus of the ▶ American Sonoran Desert provides food, moisture, and even homes for many desert animals. This cactus may grow to 15 meters and live as long as 200 years. Yet its flowers bloom only once a year – for just one night in May.

◀ When a trapdoor spider senses movement above its burrow, it will rush up and grab its **prey**.

▲ Many insects get food from these flowers and help to pollinate the plant. These plant-eating insects become food for other animals, such as birds.

▲ Cactus wrens eat insects that are attracted to the saguaro flowers.

Sudden Heavy Rains

Hot days followed by clear, cold nights form a weather pattern for many deserts. But this pattern is sometimes changed by sudden, heavy rains that bring amazing changes to the **landscape** and the plants and animals of the desert.

Seeds, buried beneath the soil, quickly sprout and take root, and some plants bloom for the first time in months, or even years. Many desert species depend on such heavy rainfalls to survive.

▲ *A heavy rainfall can change a landscape.*

◄ *Hundreds of shield shrimp eggs may hatch in a shallow pool of water. The shrimps grow, mate, and lay their own eggs, which will not hatch until the next big rainfall.*

This pink cotton plant, like many desert plants, starts growing and produces flowers and seeds in the few weeks after a heavy rainfall. But the new seeds will not grow until the next time it rains.

DESERT FACTS: A LONG DROUGHT
The Atacama desert in South America has experienced periods of more than 40 years without rain.

Desert Pools

There is very little water on the surface of deserts, but there can be a lot of **ground water** deep under the surface.

Over thousands of years, rainwater which has passed slowly down through the ground can collect in **porous** rocks or in cracks and caves. These underground water storage places are called **aquifers**.

Sometimes ground water rises to the surface, or near the surface, forming an **oasis**. An oasis can support an entire community of plants and animals.

▲ *An oasis in the Kerzaz desert, Africa.*

▲ In some desert communities, people use pumps to force water up to the surface. Then they use it to **irrigate** their crops.

People in many deserts have developed technology to bring ground water to the surface. These Fulani people in Chad use a well.

People of the Desert

Like desert animals and plants, people living in deserts have many ways of protecting themselves, keeping cool, and finding food and water.

Sometimes this means changing the desert environment to make it a better place for people to live. Whenever people change a place, they must be careful to protect the environment and preserve the natural habitats of other living things.

Many desert people wear layers of clothes to protect themselves from the heat and the burning rays of the sun.

▲ Huge amounts of water are brought into the deserts to support cities such as Aqaba, in Jordan.

▲ Some people in Tunisia survive by building their houses under the ground.

Desert Diggings

In some deserts, people have found fossils made long ago from plants, animals, and ancient humans. These fossils show scientists that some deserts used to be forests or even oceans.

Minerals lie under the surface of many parts of the Earth. People have dug huge mines in some deserts to collect diamonds, coal, and other valuable things. But this kind of activity can destroy the habitats of many animals and plants.

A diamond mine in Australia.

Fossils of ancient sea creatures show that this Australian desert was once part of the ocean floor.

Where are Deserts?

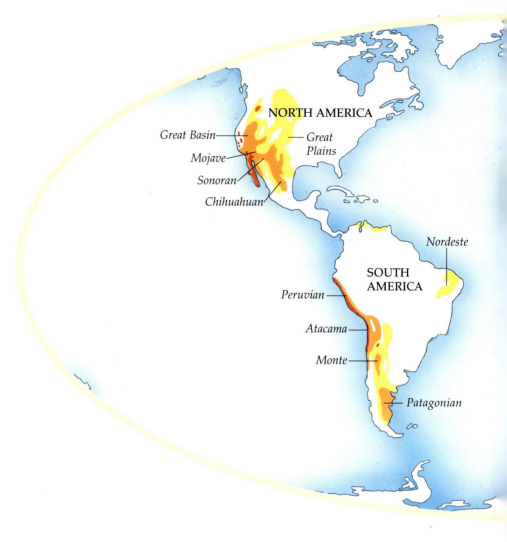

Very dry deserts where it may not rain at all for years at a time

Deserts where there is usually very little rain in a year

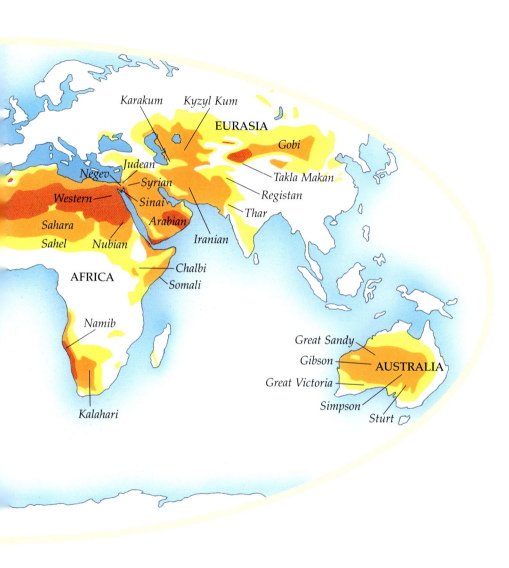

Deserts which can sometimes receive enough rain to change the land to grassland for part of the year

Who made these tracks?

A lizard's tracks, page 7

A scorpion's tracks, page 7

A fox's tracks, page 9

A dingo's tracks, page 11

A dunnart's tracks, page 17

A camel's tracks, page 17

Glossary

aquifer an area of cracks, caves, and underground rock that holds ground water (page 22)

cacti the plural of *cactus* (page 6)

cactus a family of plants which have very juicy stems, sharp spines, and no leaves (page 7)

creature a living thing, such as an animal (page 8)

enormous very large, huge (page 6)

environment a place where people, animals, or plants live and all the conditions of the land, water, and air around them (page 8)

ground water water which has collected under the ground (page 22)

habitat the place where a plant or animal normally lives (page 8)

irrigate to bring a supply of water to crops. Irrigation is used in areas that are normally too dry to grow crops. (page 23)

landscape the way an area of land looks (page 20)

nocturnal animal an animal that is active at night and sleeps during the day (page 14)

oasis (plural: *oases*) an area in the desert where ground water has come up to the surface or near the surface (page 22)

pollinate to move pollen from one flower to another. Insects and birds pollinate flowering plants as they eat nectar from the flowers. Pollination is necessary for plants to produce fruit and seeds. (page 15)

porous rocks with millions of tiny holes that water or gas can pass through (page 22)

predator an animal that hunts other animals for food (page 18)

prey an animal that is hunted by another animal (page 18)

scarce hard to find; not enough (page 4)

species (plural: *species*) a group of animals or plants of the same kind (page 8)

surface the top or outer layer of something (page 12)

survive to continue to live even in difficult conditions (page 4)

Index

animals 6–19, 22, 26, 30

aquifers 22

burrows 12, 18

cactus 7, 9, 19

food 18, 19

fossils 26–7

ground water 22

irrigation 23

minerals 26

oasis 22

people 23–6

plants 6, 7, 16, 18

predators 18

rainfall 4, 5, 12, 16, 20–22, 28–9

sand 4

temperatures 4–6, 10, 13

water 4, 6, 16–7, 20, 22–3, 25

weather 4, 11, 20–21, 28–9